THIS BOOK BELONGS TO

13-Digit ISBN: 978-1-60433-839-3
10-Digit ISBN: 1-60433-839-3

This book may be ordered by mail from the publisher. Please include $5.99 for postage and handling. Please support your local bookseller first!

Books published by Cider Mill Press Book Publishers are available at special discounts for bulk purchases in the United States by corporations, institutions, and other organizations. For more information, please contact the publisher.

Cider Mill Press Book Publishers
"Where good books are ready for press"
12 Spring Street | PO Box 454
Kennebunkport, Maine 04046
Visit us on the Web! www.cidermillpress.com

Typography: Georgia, Hoefler Text, Trajan, and Voluta Script Pro
Image Credits:
Front Endpapers:
Robert Frost Farm State Historic Site in Derry, New Hampshire. Photo courtesy of Shutterstock.
Robert Frost, head-and-shoulders portrait, facing front (between 1910 and 1920). Photo courtesy of Library of Congress.
Back Endpapers:
Robert Frost, half-length portrait, seated and facing left (1941). Photo courtesy of Library of Congress/F. Palumbo.
Winter at Bretton Woods, New Hampshire. Photo courtesy of Shutterstock.
Courtesy of Library of Congress: Front O-Band, Walter Albertin; Front endpapers; XI, Robert Frost; 30-31, Carol M. Highsmith; 57, F. Palumbo; 82; 89, Carol M. Highsmith; 105, F. Palumbo; 127, Walter Albertin; 134-135, Carol M. Highsmith; 150, Walter Albertin.
Courtesy of Shutterstock:
Front Endpapers, Jeffery M. Frank; Back Endpapers, CO Leong; 16, Robyn Mackenzie; 42-43, Mihai_Tamasila; 68-69, tete_escape; 163, Olga Popova; 179, James Kirkikis.
Courtesy of Wikimedia Commons: Cover signature.
Printed in China
1 2 3 4 5 6 7 8 9 0
First Edition

ROBERT FROST

SIGNATURE EDITION

CIDER MILL PRESS
BOOK PUBLISHERS
KENNEBUNKPORT, MAINE

Introduction

BY MAUDELLE DRISKELL

"He became a national celebrity, our nearly official poet laureate, and a great performer in the tradition of that earlier master of the literary vernacular, Mark Twain."

Confronted with this quotation, any *Jeopardy!* player would likely be able to ring in and confidently answer, "Who is Robert Frost?" Half a century after his death, Frost is still widely quoted, studied by students from middle school to grad school, and revered as America's premiere, grizzled poet. To think of Frost is to think of America—one cannot be extricated from the other.

"The Road Not Taken," arguably his most famous poem, was first published in *The Atlantic Monthly* in August 1915, and is the opening poem in his collection, *Mountain Interval* (1916). This poem, over 100 years old, still permeates American culture and stands as a testament to Frost's influence on the literary hive mind. According to David Orr in the book *The Road Not Taken: Finding America in the Poem Everyone Loves, and Almost Everyone Gets Wrong*, "This poem has become a part of the English-speaking vernacular—not just the American vernacular." Orr references a New Zealand television ad in which a heavily-accented voiceover recites the poem while a young man ponders his purchasing choice. While there's nothing earth-shattering in the production, what is highly unusual is that the advertiser assumes the audience will recognize the poem and understand it as the way in which we approach choices in our daily lives. The book declares such an assumption "stunning" and argues that the poem's "signature phrases have become so ubiquitous, so much a part of everything from coffee mugs to refrigerator magnets to graduation speeches, that it's almost possible to forget the poem is actually a poem."

Frost once claimed his goal as a poet was "to lodge a few poems where they will be hard to get rid of," and he certainly appears to have lodged his lines in granite. On a word-for-word basis, "The Road Not Taken" may be the most popular piece of literature ever written by an American.

Just two years after Frost's graduation from high school, the literary journal *The Independent* accepted his poem "My Butterfly," launching him as a professional poet with a check for $15.00. The era in which Frost matured as an author was dominated by two different approaches to poetry: the highly aestheticized verse of the canonical tradition and the rise of modernism, which pushed back against that literary inheritance. Frost chose neither of these alternatives and populated traditional poetic forms with the everyday language and imagery of New England farm communities. He wrote in the voices and cadences of real people while chronicling their daily experiences.

In 1912, after years of personal tragedy and hardship, which included the deaths of two of his young children, a failed attempt at poultry farming, and little success as a poet, he took his family to England and became acquainted with many influential poets, including Ezra Pound. His first two books, *A Boy's Will* (1913) and *North of Boston* (1914), solidly established his reputation. *North of Boston* represents the defining moment of his literary maturation. The book shows a distinct shift from his previous work, a turning away from the rhyming lyrics of *A Boy's Will*, and the development of something unmistakably new and distinctively American. Frost found his voice and, quite accidentally, America's as well.

Most of the book is written in blank verse and set in rural New England. "North of Boston" refers to a part of northern New England that was in severe decline. The population was forced to relocate, family farms were sold, and rural life was quickly disappearing. "Mending Wall" especially showcases Frost's new-found style, contrasting sharply with the writing style of his contemporaries. The diction and syntax are like those used in ordinary speech, and the poem lacks the overpowering musicality of many famous 19th century poems. The steady rhythm of iambic pentameter is not present in many of the lines, a cultivation of Frost himself. In fact, Frost said a line of poetry "will have the more charm for not being mechanically straight. We enjoy the straight crookedness of a good walking stick."

By 1920, he was one of the most celebrated poets in America, and by the last decade of his long and storied life, Frost was arguably the most prominent poet in the United States. Among his many awards and honors were four Pulitzer Prizes and the Congressional Gold Medal. Frost was asked to read a poem at the presidential inauguration of John F. Kennedy in 1961. Frost wrote a poem called "Dedication" for the occasion but couldn't read it in the bright sunlight and gusting wind. He instead recited "The Gift Outright," which Kennedy had originally asked him to read, with a revised last line. President Kennedy said, "He has bequeathed his nation a body of imperishable verse from which Americans will forever gain joy and understanding." The U.S. Senate passed a resolution, declaring that his "poems have helped to guide American thought and humor and wisdom, setting forth to our minds a reliable representation of ourselves and of all men."

Frost's poems mature with us as we encounter them throughout our lives—first in elementary school, and again and again as the years pass. Each confrontation alters both us and our understanding of the poem as we glean new depths through each reading. These poems breathe and mature alongside us.

We don't just know Frost through the published works he prepared for us. We also have the opportunity to know him through his notebooks, which he kept for more than six decades; many of which have found their way into libraries and special collections, allowing us to view them as historical artifacts and research caches. However, they served a very different purpose for Frost. Robert Fagen argues that Frost used his notebooks to work through ideas and images, revisiting them years, even decades, later to continually work toward an accretion of theories that could build a poetic approach to an expression of the ideas and themes that propel his poems.

If we have nothing else in common with Robert Frost as a poet, we have at least our notebook to jot down and record what will later inspire us.

Maudelle Driskell is the executive director of The Frost Place. She holds an MFA in poetry from Warren Wilson College and is a recipient of the Ruth Lilly Fellowship, awarded by Poetry *magazine and the Modern Language Association. Her first poetry collection,* Talismans, *was published by Hobblebush Books in 2014. She was a featured poet at Vanderbilt University's Millennial Gathering of the Writers of the New South. Her work has appeared in* Poetry, Kenyon Review, New Orleans Review, All Shook Up, The Made Thing, *and* The Cortland Review, *among others.*

Handwritten manuscript for "Stopping by Woods on a Snowy Evening" (1923)

Stopping by Woods on a Snowy Evening

Whose woods these are I think I know.
His house is in the village though.
He will not see me stopping here
To watch his woods fill up with snow.

My little horse must think it queer
To stop without a farmhouse near
Between the woods and frozen lake
The darkest evening of the year.

He gives his harness bells a shake
To ask if there is some mistake.
The only other sound's the sweep
Of easy wind and downy flake

The woods are lovely, dark and deep.
But I have promises to keep,
And miles to go before I sleep—
And miles to go before I sleep.

Robert Frost

In three words I can sum up everything I've learned about life:

IT GOES ON.

—From "Robert Frost's Secret" by Ray Josephs (*This Week Magazine*, September 1954)

Writing free verse is like playing tennis with the net down.

—From an address at Milton Academy (May 17, 1935)

FIRE AND ICE

1920

Some say the world will end in fire,
Some say in ice.
From what I've tasted of desire
I hold with those who favor fire.
But if it had to perish twice,
I think I know enough of hate
To say that for destruction ice
Is also great
And would suffice.

The acclaimed poet Robert Frost's seasonal home in rural Ripton, Vermont. From 1939 until his death in 1963, Frost spent summer and fall at this farm, where he wrote memorable poems and shared his craft at Middlebury College's Bread Loaf Writers' Conference. Photograph by Carol M. Highsmith.

Poetry begins in trivial metaphors, pretty metaphors, "grace" metaphors, and goes on to the profoundest thinking that we have. Poetry provides the one permissible way of saying one thing and meaning another.

—From "Education by Poetry," a speech delivered at Amherst College and revised for publication in *Amherst Graduates' Quarterly* (February 1931)

"We sha'n't have the place to ourselves to enjoy—
Not likely, when all the young Lorens deploy.
They'll be there to-morrow, or even to-night.
They won't be too friendly—they may be polite—
To people they look on as having no right
To pick where they're picking. But we won't complain.
You ought to have seen how it looked in the rain,
The fruit mixed with water in layers of leaves,
Like two kinds of jewels, a vision for thieves."

—From "Blueberries" (1915)

STOPPING BY WOODS ON A SNOWY EVENING

1923

Whose woods these are I think I know.
His house is in the village though;
He will not see me stopping here
To watch his woods fill up with snow.

My little horse must think it queer
To stop without a farmhouse near
Between the woods and frozen lake
The darkest evening of the year.

He gives his harness bells a shake
To ask if there is some mistake.
The only other sound's the sweep
Of easy wind and downy flake.

The woods are lovely, dark and deep,
But I have promises to keep,
And miles to go before I sleep,
And miles to go before I sleep.

How many times it thundered before Franklin took the hint! How many apples fell on Newton's head before he took the hint!

NATURE IS ALWAYS HINTING AT US.

It hints over and over again. And suddenly we take the hint.

—From *Lives of the Poets: The Story of One Thousand Years of English and American Poetry* by Louis Untermeyer (1959)

From following walls I never lift my eye,
Except at night to places in the sky
Where showers of charted meteors let fly.

Some may know what they seek in school and church,
And why they seek it there; for what I search
I must go measuring stone walls, perch on perch;

—From "A Star in a Stone-Boat" (1927)

Robert Frost, half-length portrait, facing front, looking down, and reading, photographed by F. Palumbo for New York World-Telegram *(1941)*

DUST OF SNOW

1923

The way a crow
Shook down on me
The dust of snow
From a hemlock tree

Has given my heart
A change of mood
And saved some part
Of a day I had rued.

TO EARTHWARD

1923

Love at the lips was touch
As sweet as I could bear;
And once that seemed too much;
I lived on air

That crossed me from sweet things,
The flow of—was it musk
From hidden grapevine springs
Downhill at dusk?

I had the swirl and ache
From sprays of honeysuckle
That when they're gathered shake
Dew on the knuckle.

I craved strong sweets, but those
Seemed strong when I was young;
The petal of the rose
It was that stung.

Now no joy but lacks salt,
That is not dashed with pain
And weariness and fault;
I crave the stain

Of tears, the aftermark
Of almost too much love,
The sweet of bitter bark
And burning clove.

When stiff and sore and scarred
I take away my hand
From leaning on it hard
In grass and sand,

The hurt is not enough:
I long for weight and strength
To feel the earth as rough
To all my length.

A poet never takes notes.

YOU NEVER TAKE NOTES IN A LOVE AFFAIR.

—From an interview with Cecil Day Lewis (*BBC*, September 13, 1957); transcript published in "It Takes a Hero to Make a Poem" (*Claremont Quarterly*, Spring 1958)

The sidelong glance is what you depend on. You look at your author but you

KEEP THE TAIL OF YOUR EYE ON WHAT IS HAPPENING

over and above your author in your own mind and nature.

—Advice on writing an essay in a letter to his eldest daughter, Lesley Frost Ballantine, from *The Letters of Robert Frost, Volume 1* (2014)

Outbuilding on the grounds of the Robert Frost Stone House in Shaftsbury, Vermont, which became a museum in 2002. Robert Frost came to Shaftsbury in 1920 at the height of his career as a poet. While living here, Frost wrote two books of poetry, won his first Pulitzer Prize, and penned perhaps his most famous poem, "Stopping by Woods on a Snowy Evening." Photograph by Carol M. Highsmith.

BLUE-BUTTERFLY DAY

1923

It is blue-butterfly day here in spring,
And with these sky-flakes down in flurry on flurry
There is more unmixed color on the wing
Than flowers will show for days unless they hurry.

But these are flowers that fly and all but sing:
And now from having ridden out desire
They lie closed over in the wind and cling
Where wheels have freshly sliced the April mire.

I never write except with a writing board. I've never had a table in my life. And I use all sorts of things. Write on the sole of my shoe.

—From "Robert Frost, The Art of Poetry No. 2"
(*The Paris Review*, Issue 24, Summer-Fall 1960)

Robert Frost, half-length portrait, seated and facing left, photographed by F. Palumbo for New York World-Telegram *(1941)*

It is only

A MOMENT HERE AND A MOMENT THERE

that the greatest writer has.

—From *Robert Frost: The Trial by Existence*
by Elizabeth Shepley Sergeant (1960)

A complete poem is
one where an
EMOTION
FINDS THE
THOUGHT
and the thought finds
the words.

—From a letter to Louis Untermeyer (January 1, 1919), published in *The Letters of Robert Frost to Louis Untermeyer* (1963)

Robert Frost poses with his birthday cake on his 85th birthday, photographed by Walter Albertin for New York World-Telegram *(1959)*

Always fall in with what you're asked to accept.

TAKE WHAT IS GIVEN, AND MAKE IT OVER YOUR WAY.

My aim in life has always been to hold my own with whatever's going. Not against: with.

—From "The Fearless Wisdom of Robert Frost" (*Vogue*, March 14, 1963)

The Robert Frost Stone House. Photograph by Carol M. Highsmith.

The right reader of a good poem

CAN TELL THE MOMENT IT STRIKES HIM

that he has taken an immortal wound—that he will never get over it.

—From "The Poetry of Amy Lowell," (*The Christian Science Monitor*, May 16, 1925)

PLOWMEN

1923

A plow, they say, to plow the snow.
They cannot mean to plant it, no–
Unless in bitterness to mock
At having cultivated rock.

Robert Frost at 85, photographed by Walter Albertin for New York World-Telegram *(1959)*

“Men work together,”
I told him from the heart,
“Whether they work together or apart.”

—From “The Tuft of Flowers” (1913)

Robert Frost stamp (c. 1974)

U.S. 10¢
Robert Frost
AMERICAN POET

Robert Frost coupled poetry and power, for he saw poetry as the means of saving power from itself.

WHEN POWER LEADS MEN TOWARDS ARROGANCE, POETRY REMINDS HIM OF HIS LIMITATIONS.

When power narrows the areas of man's concern, poetry reminds him of the richness and diversity of his existence. When power corrupts, poetry cleanses. For art establishes the basic human truth which must serve as the touchstone of our judgment.

—John F. Kennedy, at the Groundbreaking for the Robert Frost Library at Amherst College (October 26, 1963)

NOTHING GOLD CAN STAY

1923

Nature's first green is gold,
Her hardest hue to hold.
Her early leaf's a flower;
But only so an hour.
Then leaf subsides to leaf,
So Eden sank to grief,
So dawn goes down to day.
Nothing gold can stay.

The grave of Robert Frost and his wife rests at a cemetery in Bennington, Vermont. It reads "I had a lover's quarrel with the world," which is the final line of his poem "The Lesson for Today" (1942).

About Cider Mill Press Book Publishers

Good ideas ripen with time. From seed to harvest, Cider Mill Press brings fine reading, information, and entertainment together between the covers of its creatively crafted books. Our Cider Mill bears fruit twice a year, publishing a new crop of titles each spring and fall.

CIDER MILL PRESS

BOOK PUBLISHERS

"Where Good Books Are Ready for Press"

Visit us on the Web at
www.cidermillpress.com
or write to us at
PO Box 454
12 Spring St.
Kennebunkport, Maine 04046